Better Homes and Gardens®

The Surprising Pockets

"When is Mrs. Kelsey coming to baby-sit, Mommy?" asked Tweetums.

"Mrs. Kelsey moved away, remember?" Tweetums' mother said. "Mrs. Featherby is coming tonight."

Tweetums frowned. "I don't want a new baby-sitter. Mrs. Kelsey and I always had fun together."

"I'm sure you'll like Mrs. Featherby," Tweetums' mother said, looking at the clock. "You still have time before she comes. Why don't you go play with your friends for a while?"

When Tweetums got to the willow tree where her friends always played, Bruno and Max were the only ones there.

"Hi, guys! Guess what? I'm having a new baby-sitter tonight," Tweetums said. "Mrs. Featherby."

"Are you kidding? Mrs. Featherby isn't any fun!" said Bruno.

"Why not?" Tweetums asked.

"She isn't *anything* like Mrs. Kelsey!" Bruno exclaimed.

"I always had fun with Mrs. Kelsey," muttered Tweetums.

"Mrs. Featherby doesn't even read bedtime stories," said Bruno.

"Really?" Max said. "I never heard of a baby-sitter who didn't read bedtime stories."

"But I have *Night-Night Birdie* read to me every night," Tweetums cried. "I want a baby-sitter just like Mrs. Kelsey!" Then she ran all the way home just as fast as she could.

"Please, please find another baby-sitter, Mommy!" Tweetums said. "Bruno says Mrs. Featherby isn't any fun at all."

Tweetums' mother looked surprised. "I can't imagine why Bruno said that. Mrs. Featherby seems very nice. I'm sure you'll have fun with her."

Tweetums' father gave Tweetums a hug. "Let's give Mrs. Featherby a chance, OK? You can't believe everything you hear."

"But, Daddy . . . " It was too late. There was a knock on the door. Tweetums' mother opened it and there stood Mrs. Featherby.

Mrs. Featherby didn't look like any baby-sitter Tweetums had ever seen. She didn't look like *anybody* Tweetums had ever seen. She had pockets everywhere. Tweetums had never seen so many pockets.

Tweetums' mother kissed Tweetums good-bye. "Be good for Mrs. Featherby. I'm sure you'll have a good time."

Tweetums didn't say anything for a while. She just kept looking at Mrs. Featherby. Finally she asked, "Why do you have all those funny pockets?"

"Well, you never know when you might need a little of this or a lot of that," Mrs. Featherby said.

Mrs. Featherby started pulling all kinds of
things from her pockets. She showed
Tweetums how a piece of fuzzy yarn made a
pretty hair bow. She gave Tweetums a
necklace she had made from buttons of all
sizes, shapes, and colors. Then Mrs.
Featherby held an old newspaper over
Tweetums' head and explained how it
worked as an umbrella.

"I'm getting hungry," Mrs. Featherby said
as she patted one of her pockets. "Let's go
make something to eat."

Tweetums followed Mrs. Featherby into
the kitchen. "Sandwiches are the only thing
I like to eat," Tweetums said.

"The *only* thing?" Mrs. Featherby looked surprised. "Well, that doesn't sound like fun. Isn't it boring eating the same thing all the time?"

"Well, maybe a little," Tweetums said.

Tweetums watched Mrs. Featherby pull fruits and vegetables and a hunk of cheese out of her pockets. "I don't like fruits and vegetables," said Tweetums firmly.

"You've never had fruits and vegetables the way I fix them," Mrs. Featherby said. "I think you'll like these just fine."

Mrs. Featherby began slicing and chopping. Then she put some pieces together on a plate and handed it to Tweetums. "Ta-da! How do you like it?"

"What is it?" Tweetums asked.

"You think of a name," Mrs. Featherby said, as she started another creation.

Tweetums looked puzzled. "Could it be a wibble?"

Mrs. Featherby laughed. "I think that's exactly what it is. Why don't you try making one now."

WIBBLE

GLEEBIE

Before long, Mrs. Featherby and Tweetums had put together a whole bunch of creatures. Then they had a delicious dinner of wibbles, gleebies, yeekers, and zoggs.

"That was yummy," said Tweetums, finishing her last bite.

Mrs. Featherby looked at her watch. "My, my," she said. "It's time for bed."

YEEKER

ZOGG

"Will you read a bedtime story?"
Tweetums asked. "I have *Night-Night Birdie*
read to me every night."

"The same story every night?" asked Mrs.
Featherby. "That doesn't sound like fun!"
She sat down in the rocking chair beside
Tweetums' bed. "Let's make up a story
instead."

"Oh, I can't," Tweetums said.

"Of course you can," answered Mrs.
Featherby. "All it takes is a little
imagination. And you have plenty of that."

"I do?" Tweetums asked.

"Sure. Here's a magic storytelling cap."
Mrs. Featherby pulled a purple cap out of
her biggest pocket and put it on Tweetums'
head. "I'll help you get started: 'There once
was a little girl name Tweetums . . .' "

"This story is about *me*?" asked
Tweetums.

Mrs. Featherby nodded. ". . . and more than anything else in the world, Tweetums wanted to be . . . what?"

"Big!" Tweetums said. "She wanted to be bigger than all of her friends—even bigger than Max and Bruno."

"How do you think Tweetums could make herself grow big?" Mrs. Featherby asked.

"I don't know," said Tweetums. "Maybe she ate some special growing food."

Mrs. Featherby rocked back and forth in her chair. "I wonder what kind of food that could be?"

Tweetums giggled, "Wibbles, gleebies, yeekers, and zoggs! And the more of them she ate, the taller she grew."

Mrs. Featherby smiled and rocked.

Tweetums went on with her story.

"Tweetums grew taller than her mother and father. Soon she was taller than the roof of her house. Her legs grew so long, she could walk to school in only three steps."

Tweetums went on and on and Mrs. Featherby sat listening, rocking, and smiling. Finally Tweetums fell asleep and had wonderful dreams about being big.

The next morning, Tweetums' mother
pulled up the window shade. "Tweetums,
wake up. It's time for breakfast."

"Mommy? Where's Mrs. Featherby?"

"She left last night when we got home.
Did you have a nice time?"

"Oh, yes! We had a lot of fun," Tweetums
said. "She was great. I'm going to tell Bruno
he was wrong." Tweetums made herself a
wibble for breakfast and then went outside
to find Bruno.

Max and Bruno were on the sidewalk,
playing marbles. Max looked up. "Hi,
Tweetums! How was Mrs. Featherby?"

"She was lots of fun," Tweetums said.

"Really?" asked Bruno.

Tweetums told them about everything they
had done.

"Mrs. Featherby sounds great," said Max. "Why wasn't she any fun when she baby-sat for you, Bruno?"

Bruno scuffed his feet on the sidewalk. "Well, she didn't exactly baby-sit for me."

"For a friend of yours?" Max asked.

"It was sort of a friend . . . of a friend . . . of a friend," Bruno mumbled.

"My daddy said you can't believe everything you hear," Tweetums said. "And he was right."

"I have to go home now," Bruno said suddenly. "Bye!"

"What about our game?" Max asked.

"Maybe later. My dad and mom are going out tonight and I want them to get Mrs. Featherby to baby-sit for me!"

Fruity Creatures

Build a silly creature out of fruit. Then give it a funny name.

What you'll need...

- 1 small red apple
- Cutting board
- Paring knife
- Salad plate
- Peanut butter or cream cheese
- 2 raisins or currants

1 Have an adult cut the apple for you. On a cutting board use the paring knife to cut the apple in half and remove the core. Save 1 apple half for another use. Place the other apple half, cut side down, on the cutting board. Cut 2 slices off each side of the apple (see photo).

2 For the body, put the large uncut portion of the apple half on a salad plate. Place 2 apple slices next to 1 side of the body. Push the slices away from the body and a little to the back (see photo). Place remaining slices on other side of the body the same way.

3 For one eye, put some peanut butter on a raisin (see photo). Place the raisin on the body. Repeat with another raisin.

If you like, create other kinds of Fruity Creatures (see Creature Cousins on page 32).

Puppet Storybook

Make a puppet person and put it on every page of your very own storybook.

What you'll need...

- Markers or crayons
- 3 or 4 lightweight paper plates or pieces of construction paper
- Scissors
- White crafts glue or tape
- 1 jumbo craft stick
- Paper punch
- 2 pieces of yarn or string, each about 8 inches long

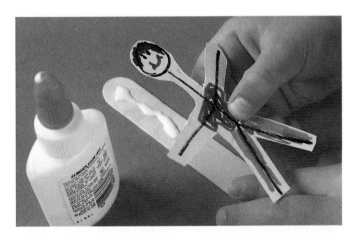

1 For the puppet, use markers to draw a picture of yourself on a paper plate. Use scissors to cut out the picture. Glue the picture to the top half of the craft stick (see photo).

2 On the other paper plates, draw pictures of places you like, such as your backyard, school, or the zoo (see photo).

  Have an adult cut a slit about 1 inch wide in each plate. Slide the craft stick with the puppet through the slit. Move the puppet from page to page as you tell a story.

3 Use a paper punch to punch 2 holes in the top or side of each paper plate. Stack the plates on top of each other so the holes match up. Push 1 piece of yarn through 1 set of holes. Tie it with a knot (see photo). Repeat with other piece of yarn and other set of holes.

Big Blocks

Pretend you're very tall when you walk on these paper-carton blocks.

What you'll need...

- 1 pencil or crafts knife
- Two ½-gallon paper cartons
- Tape
- 2 pieces of string or yarn, each about 1 yard long
- Newspaper

1 With adult help, use a pencil to punch a hole near the center of an edge of 1 long side of 1 paper carton (see photo). Turn the carton over. Punch another hole opposite the first hole. Repeat with the other paper carton.

2 Wrap a piece of tape around 1 end of 1 piece of the string. Push the taped end of the string through 1 hole (see photo). Put your hand inside the carton. Pull the end of the string through the carton and put it through the hole on the other side. Tie the ends of the string together. Repeat with the other carton.

3 Wad up several sheets of newspaper and stuff them into 1 carton. Pack the paper tightly into the carton until it's almost full (see photo). Close the carton and push the top to one side so it's flat. Tape it down. Repeat with the other carton.

Fruity Creatures

What's your favorite fruit? Would it make a good Fruity Creature? Here are some more ideas you can use to make fun fruit salads like the ones on page 26.

Creature Cousins: For the bodies, use fruit such as fresh or canned peach, apricot, or pear halves. Decorate the creatures with chow mein noodles, mixed dried fruit bits, apple slices, slivered almonds or other nuts, or small pieces of cheese.

For vegetable creatures use cucumbers, zucchini, carrots, celery, or broccoli.

Puppet Storybook

Parents: Many children thoroughly enjoy making up their own stories, but they might need a little help getting started. Try this storytelling activity to challenge their creativity.

Fill a paper or plastic bag or a pillowcase with a combination of several small stuffed animals, dolls, or other small toys. Have one child pull an animal from the bag. Then you can start the story with "Once upon a time there was a. . . ." Both you and the children can build on the story as each child pulls another animal or toy from the bag.

When the story ends, ask your children if they want to make Puppet Storybooks about the new story they just made up.

Big Blocks

Do you like pretending to be big? How could you pretend to be little? Look at the pictures below.
- Point to the big house. Point to the little house.
- Point to the full glass. Point to the empty glass.
- Which box is open? Which box is closed?
- Which person is tall? Which person is short?

BETTER HOMES AND GARDENS® BOOKS
Editor: Gerald M. Knox   Art Director: Ernest Shelton   Managing Editor: David A. Kirchner
Family Life Editor: Sharyl Heiken
THE SURPRISING POCKETS
Editors: Jennifer Darling and Sandra Granseth   Graphic Designers: Harijs Priekulis and Linda Vermie
Project Manager: Liz Anderson
Contributing Writer: Jane Stanley   Contributing Illustrator: Buck Jones
Contributing Color Artist: Sue Fitzpatrick Cornelison   Contributing Photographer: Scott Little

Have BETTER HOMES AND GARDENS® magazine delivered to your door.
For information, write to: ROBERT AUSTIN, P.O. BOX 4536, DES MOINES, IA 50336